Copyright © Joy Berry, 2020
Reprinted by permission. Originally Published 2010

The statements and opinions expressed in this work are solely those of the author and do not reflect the thoughts or opinions of the publisher.

Every effort has been made to trace the copyright holder(s) and obtain permission to reproduce all elements of this material.

All rights reserved. No part of this book may be reproduced or used in any manner without the prior written permission of the copyright owner, except for the use of brief quotations in a book review. For inquiries or to request permission, contact the publisher at rights@lemurpress.com

ISBN 978-1-63617-030-5

Published by Lemur Press
lemurpress.com

LEMUR PRESS

I love my friends!

I like to spend time with them.

I like to play with them.

I treat my friends the way I want them to treat me.

I am kind to my friends.

I try not to do anything that would hurt them.

My friends and I take turns deciding what to do.

Sometimes we do what they want to do.

Sometimes we do what I want to do.

My friends and I share things.

If there is only one thing that both of us want to play with, we take turns using it.

If there is only one thing to eat, we divide it, and each of us gets some.

Sometimes my friends come to my house.

I put away the things I do not want to share with my friends.

I share all of my other things with them.

Sometimes I play with my friends at their houses.

I only play with the things my friends want to share with me.

I help clean up any messes that we make.

Sometimes my friends hurt me.

I ask them to stop.

If they don't stop, I walk away until they agree to play nicely with me.

If my friends and I are hurting each other, we stop what we are doing.

We say that we are sorry for hurting each other.

We try never to hurt each other again.

My friends are fun to play with.

They make me happy.

I love my friends!

www.ingramcontent.com/pod-product-compliance
Lightning Source LLC
Chambersburg PA
CBHW081413070526
44583CB00020B/2786